Living in
India

Ruth Thomson
Photography by David Hampton

W
FRANKLIN WATTS
LONDON•SYDNEY

First published in 2002 by
Franklin Watts,
96 Leonard Street,
London EC2A 4XD

Franklin Watts Australia,
56 O'Riordan Street,
Alexandria, NSW 2015

Copyright © Franklin Watts 2002

Series editor: Ruth Thomson
Series designer: Edward Kinsey
Additional photographs: Rachel Hamdi pages 7,
8, 9, 11(tr, bl, br) 13(tl), 18(b), 19(br), 22(r),
24(tr); Leo Thomson, 6, 14(tl, b) 15(tl, c, b),
16(tl), 19(tr), 21(cl), 24(br), 25(br), 26(b), 27(r),
29(bl), 30(t); Laraine Welch 4(tl)

A CIP catalogue record for this book is
available from the British Library.
Dewey classification 915.4

ISBN 0 7496 4641 1

Printed in Malaysia

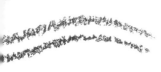

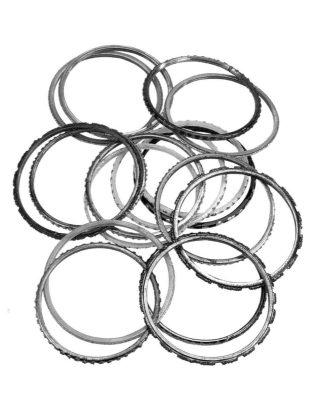

Contents

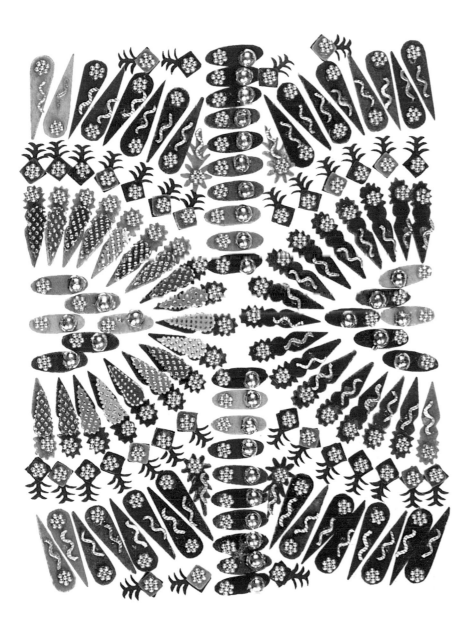

This is India

India is a country of immense variety. The high, snowy Himalayas in the north give way to rich, flat farmland, watered by the River Ganges.

South of the plains, the land rises into the Deccan plateau, with forested hills on either side.

△**Big cities**
Cities are densely populated. Mumbai, the largest, has more than 15 million inhabitants.

△**The Himalayas**
The highest mountain range in the world separates northern India from China, Bhutan and Nepal.

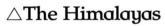

▷**The desert**
Rain rarely falls in the hot, vast Thar Desert, in the north-west.

Fact Box

Capital: Delhi
Population: 1 billion
Official languages: Hindi, English and 13 other languages
Main religions: Hinduism, Islam, Christianity, Sikhism, Buddhism, Jainism
Highest mountain: Nanda Devi (7816m)
Longest river: Ganges (2480km)
Biggest cities: Mumbai, Calcutta, Delhi, Chennai, Hyderabad, Bangalore
Currency: Rupees

Disputed
territory
KASHMIR &
JAMMU

CHINA

PUNJAB

PAKISTAN

Thar Desert

Himalayas

Nanda Devi ▲
● **Delhi**

NEPAL

BHUTAN

R. Brahmaputra

Amber
● **Agra**

Jaipur ●

**Fatehpur
Sikri**

R. Ganges

BANGLADESH

BURMA

GUJARAT

R. Tapti

Calcutta ●
(Kalkota)

**Mumbai
(Bombay)** ●

Deccan Plateau

R. Godavi

Hyderabad ●

R. Krishna

Bay of Bengal

Goa ●

Western Ghats

Indian Ocean

KERALA

Andaman Islands

Bangalore
● **Chennai (Madras)**

Nicobar Islands

▷**A fertile land**
Waterways criss-
cross the region
of Kerala, in the
south-west.
Rice, coconuts
and cashew nuts
grow here.

▷**The coastline**
India has more than 9,000 km of
coastline. Goa, on the west coast, is
famous for its long, sandy beaches.

Religions

Religion plays an important part in everyday life. Over 80% of the population practise Hinduism, one of the oldest religions in the world. Hindus worship in temples and often have a shrine in their homes where they pray every day.

There are also millions of Muslims and many Christians, Sikhs and Buddhists.

△**A priest (*Brahmin*)**
A priest performs all the ceremonies in a Hindu temple.

△**A Hindu temple (*mandir*)**
The temple houses the sacred image of a god. This richly carved temple is in south India.

◁**Gifts of worship**
At this temple entrance, Hindus can buy flowers, coconut, bananas and incense, as gifts for the gods.

▷At the mosque (*masjid*)

Muslims pray five times a day, at home or at work. On Fridays (their holy day), they often go to the mosque at midday. They pray together and listen to a sermon.

▽Learning the Koran

Muslim boys come to the mosque to learn the Koran, the Muslim holy book, by heart.

△A Sikh temple (*gurdwara*)

Inside a Sikh temple is a prayer hall, a kitchen and sometimes a school or a hostel. After worship, Sikhs often share a meal together.

Delhi – the capital

Delhi is India's third largest city. It has two main parts. Old Delhi is a walled city. It was the capital of the Mughal emperors, who once ruled India. They built many mosques, a fort and other monuments.

▽**The great mosque**
The Jama Masjid is the largest mosque in India. 25,000 people can pray together in its enormous courtyard.

△**Kutab Minar**
This tower of victory was built by Muslims who ruled Delhi in the 12th century.

▷**Chandi Chowk**
People throng this main shopping street and the alleys nearby, lined with shops selling food, spices and perfumes.

▽Raj Path (Kingsway)

Government buildings line the main road of New Delhi. The President's residence is at one end of it. There is a triumphal arch at the other end.

▽India Gate

The arch bears names of Indian Army soldiers who died in the First World War (1914-1918).

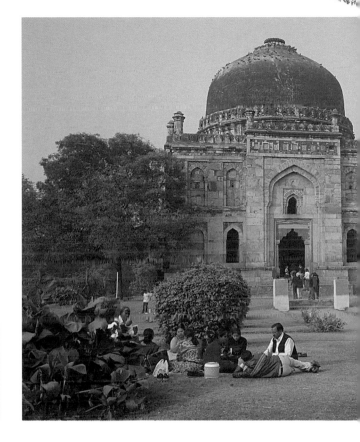

New Delhi

In the early 20th century, when the British ruled India, they decided to make Delhi their new capital. A British architect, Sir Edwin Lutyens, designed a spacious new city, with wide, tree-lined roads, grand government buildings, palaces for important people and bungalows for officials and their families.

△Lodi Gardens

Delhi has numerous parks and gardens where people stroll and picnic.

Famous sights

India has an ancient history. Many of its Hindu temples, cave carvings and holy cities are thousands of years old.

The Mughal emperors built many magnificent palaces, forts and tombs, which have now become major tourist attractions.

△**The River Ganges**
The Ganges is sacred to the Hindus. They make pilgrimages to the river and bathe in its waters.

*Entrance tickets
to some famous sights*

▷**The Taj Mahal, Agra**
The Mughal emperor, Shah Jahan, was heart-broken when his wife died. He built this beautiful marble tomb for her, which took 21 years to complete.

◁**Palace of the Winds**
This building overlooks the main street of the city of Jaipur. Royal ladies watched the world through its airy windows, without being seen themselves.

▷**An observatory**
These structures in Jaipur are astronomical instruments. They measure the positions of the sun or stars.

◁**An elephant ride**
Taking a ride on an elephant is a treat for visitors who come to visit the fort at Amber.

▷**Fatehpur Sikri**
Akbar, a Mughal ruler, built this city as his capital. Abandoned after 14 years, it is perfectly preserved in the dry heat.

11

Living in cities

India has many large, sprawling cities. They are centres for big business, technology and modern factories.

Cities are growing year by year, as millions of poor villagers move there. Some find work as labourers or in factories, or drive auto rickshaws.

△Crowded streets
City streets are packed, day and night, with pedestrians as well as cars, taxis, bicycles, scooters and carts.

▷Shanty towns
People who have come from the country cannot always afford to rent homes. Many have built shacks from scrap materials, in areas known as shanty towns.

△City flats
In some cities, such as Mumbai and Bangalore, the better-off live in modern, high-rise blocks of flats.

▽Factories
There are hundreds of factories on the outskirts of cities. Huge ones make TVs, textiles or cars. Others make household goods.

△Electricity
It is hard for cities to produce enough electricity for everyone. There are often power cuts.

△A city laundry
At this huge open-air laundry, clothes are washed by hand in large concrete tubs.

◁At your service
The city pavements are crowded with people selling goods or offering services, such as shining shoes or letter writing.

Living in villages

Three out of four Indians live in villages, surrounded by fields and often several miles from a road.

Families live in small, detached houses made of brick, concrete or dried clay mixed with straw. These may have a room for sleeping and another for cooking. Some bigger houses have an enclosed courtyard.

△Cooking fuel
Women press cow dung into flat pats and leave them to dry. These can then be used as fuel.

△Fetching water
Villages have a well or water pump, where people fetch water daily. Nearly half of all villages now have piped water.

◁ Village roads
Village roads are often unpaved. Cars and trucks are rare sights.

Henna powder

Candles

Matches

Batteries

Soap

A village barber

A village shop

△The village shop
A village shop usually sells basic household goods like these, and perhaps sweets, bottled drinks and a few food items.

◁Washing clothes
Many village women take their laundry to a nearby river or stream. Sometimes, they use a specially built washing spot (*ghat*).

Village work

Most villagers are farmers who own small plots of land. They grow cereals (wheat in the north and rice in the south), pulses (chick peas, lentils and beans) and vegetables for their own use.

Richer famers grow tea, sugar cane, cotton and jute as cash crops.

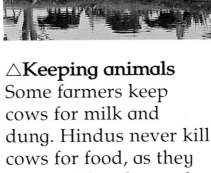

△**Keeping animals**
Some farmers keep cows for milk and dung. Hindus never kill cows for food, as they are considered sacred.

△**Animal power**
Many farmers use bullocks to pull their ploughs and carts. Tractors are used in richer areas.

▷**Vegetables**
These are some of the vegetables that farmers may grow.

Okra

Beans

Pumpkin

Aubergines

Chillies

Bitter gourd

Potatoes

▷Fishing

People in coastal villages catch and sell fish. They use traditional wooden boats as well as modern trawlers.

▽Cottage industries

Some villagers are craft workers. They work at home making metal utensils, clay pots or cloth. Parents pass on skills to their children.

▽Harvest time

People with no land of their own work on other people's farms.

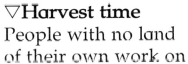

17

Shopping

Most shops are small and open-fronted. There are also numerous street sellers, who sell their goods from a spot on the pavement or from a barrow.

In cities, there are specialist markets with rows of stalls selling similar goods, such as sweets, cloth or jewellery.

△**The market**
Towns have a daily or weekly fruit and vegetable market. Meat is sold in a separate market.

△**Street sellers**
Hawkers wander city streets, selling small portable things, such as sunglasses, pens or knives.

◁**Groceries**
Few foods are pre-packaged. Nuts, grains, pulses and dried fruits are sold loose, like this.

An electrical goods shop

A sweet stall

Sweets

Bangles

A sari shop

A bangle shop

Prices

In many shops, prices are not fixed. People bargain hard for the goods they want to buy.

△**Useful services**
Services, such as barbers and dentists, are often above shops.

On the move

Major towns and cities are increasingly clogged up with motor traffic. Only the very wealthy can afford cars, but many people use mopeds and scooters.

In country areas, people use bikes and bullock carts, or walk.

△**Bullock carts**
The cheapest form of transport, for both people and goods, is a bullock cart.

△**A cheap ride**
This auto rickshaw is a quick and cheap kind of taxi. People use one for short rides in towns.

▷**Air pollution**
Dense motor traffic causes air pollution in the bigger cities.

△**Bicycle rickshaws**
In small towns, bicycles and bicycle rickshaws are common.

20

▽On the buses
Local buses are cheap, but slow and crowded. They stop at every small place. Express buses travel between big towns.

◁Trucks
Colourful painted trucks carry goods across the country, especially to and from places where there is no railway.

Bus tickets

Long-distance travel
Indians regularly travel a long way to visit holy places, to stay with relatives or to go to weddings. Railways link all the major cities. Journeys between distant towns can take several days and nights.

△Trains
Local trains bring workers into the cities every day.

21

Family life

In some parts of India, lots of relatives live together in one big family. The oldest man is the head of the household. When a woman marries, she moves into the family home of her husband and helps with the work of the household.

◁**A joint family**
A household may consist of two grandparents, several sons, their wives and a number of children.

△**City families**
In cities, where living space is more cramped, young people are beginning to set up smaller family homes.

◁Women's work

Women do the household jobs. They cook, clean, fetch water and firewood, wash clothes and care for children.

▽Family size

Rural families are generally larger than city families. Parents hope their children will help with the farm work.

◁Men's work

Men do most of the farm work. During harvest and other busy times, when extra hands are needed, women may work in the fields as well.

Village families

In farming families, women and men usually do very different tasks. Children often help with everyday tasks from a young age.

In craftworking families, men and women may both work, doing the weaving or clothprinting.

Time to eat

The food people eat varies from region to region. In the Punjab, many people eat meat and several sorts of breads. In south India, people flavour dishes with coconut and eat them with rice.

On the coast, people eat fish dishes. In Gujarat, people serve many different dishes together, on a tray called a *thali*.

△A spice stall
In many parts of India food is flavoured with a mixture of spices. These are freshly ground for every meal.

▷Hand-made sweets
People buy sweets, like these, as presents and for festivals. They are made with ghee (a type of butter), sugar and creamy milk, and flavoured with nuts.

△Fresh vegetables
Many Hindus are vegetarians. They make dishes with vegetables, pulses and rice or bread. Some eat chicken and fish as well.

A hand-made sweet stall

◁**Fruit snacks**
Some food sellers prepare slices of fresh peeled fruit. Others make fruit juices.

▷**Fast food**
This food seller cooks his snacks in a big pan (*karai*) of sizzling oil.

Eating out

Cheap street snacks are found everywhere. Stalls sell spicy fried savouries, grilled kebabs or plates of hot curry, *dal* (a lentil dish) and rice.

Restaurants cook dishes of their area. Some sell only vegetarian food. Muslim restaurants serve lamb and chicken dishes.

△**A snack stall**
Some stalls are mobile kitchen barrows.

School time

Children go to primary school between the ages of 6 and 14. They have lessons in maths, social studies, drawing, games and useful handcrafts, as well as reading and writing.

Wealthy parents can send their children to well-equipped, private schools. In poor village schools, pupils sit on the floor and write on slates.

△**School uniform**
Many schoolchildren wear smart school uniform.

▷**In the classroom**
There are about 35 pupils in a class. In some places, there are too many pupils for a school, so the children go in shifts.

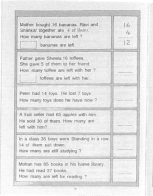

Maths book

Social studies books

*Exercise book
protected
with brown
paper*

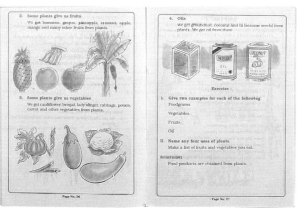

◁School books

Some schools teach in English, one of India's two official languages. They use books like these. To go to university, students must be able to read, write and speak in English.

△Secondary schools

Most secondary schools are single-sex and fee-paying.
Far more boys go to secondary schools than girls.

School or work?

Primary school is free, but not all children go to school. Just over half the population can read and write. In rural areas especially, families may keep girls at home to look after younger children, while boys work alongside their fathers.

Having fun

△**Music**
The biggest selling albums are songs from films.

▷**The films**
Most films are a mixture of dance, song, romance and adventure. They last three or four hours.

Cinema tickets

Cinema is the most popular form of entertainment in India. More films are made there than anywhere else in the world – nearly 700 a year. The film industry in Mumbai is known as Bollywood.

Videos are now also widely available, so people may watch films at home.

△**Cinema news**
Film magazines have interviews and gossip about film stars.

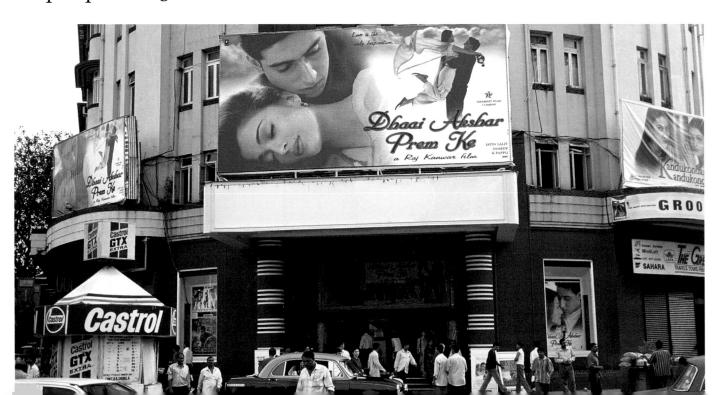

28

◁**Cricket**
Indians enjoy cricket.
Children set up a game
on any spare patch of land.
India's national team plays
in test matches against other
countries.

◁**Watching television**
Even in remote country
areas, households with
electricity can watch
satellite television.

▷**Fireworks**
There are many
festivals throughout
the year. Fireworks are
often part of the
colourful celebrations.

Going further

Indian spices

Make a collection of spices, such as ginger, turmeric, cumin, coriander, chilli, fenugreek, cardamom, mustard seed and cinnamon. Look in an Indian cookbook and find out how they are used.

Find out what part of a plant each one comes from. Is it a root, a seed, the bark or a leaf? Discover how and where each spice grows. Is it a tree, vine, bush or flowering plant?

The Ramayana

The Ramayana is an long and ancient story about Prince Rama and his battle with Ravana, the many-headed demon king, who kidnaps Rama's wife Sita.

Find out more about this story and draw a scene from it. Find out which Hindu festivals celebrate events from the Ramayana.

Indian crafts

Choose an Indian craft, such as jewellery, metalwork, pottery, embroidery or weaving. Make a booklet about it.

Find out what sort of things the craftworkers make and what tools and materials they use. Illustrate your book with some of their designs and patterns.

Useful websites

www.india-crafts.com
www.babloo.com
http://indiabykids.com/ibk
www.searchindia.com

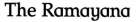

Glossary

Cash crop A crop that is grown for sale and not as food for the farmer.

Cottage industry A small-scale industry, often based in people's homes.

Currency The money used by a country.

Curry A meat, fish or vegetable dish flavoured with spices.

Drought A long period where there is very little rainfall or none at all.

Henna powder A green powder made from crushed leaves. It is mixed with water to make a red dye, which women use to paint patterns on their hands and feet.

Jute A plant fibre used for making sacks and mats.

Mughal The Muslim dynasty of emperors, who ruled over the north of India from the 16th to the 18th century.

Observatory A building or place where astronomers can study the sun, moon and stars.

Plain An area of open, flat land.

Plateau A high area of flat land.

Population The total number of people living in a place.

Pollution Damage to the environment caused by chemicals, fumes and other waste products from either cars, industry or farming.

Shanty town An area of unplanned housing on city outskirts without power or water supplies, sewers or rubbish collection. Homes are made from scrap materials such as wood, corrugated iron, sacking and plastic.

Spices Sharp, hot or fragrant food substances used for flavouring food.

Tomb A grave where someone is buried.

Trawler A fishing boat with a huge bag-net for dragging along the sea-bed.

Index